Freeze Out Crooks

FOREWORD

This book is in no way intended to offer legal advice: it merely describes the benefits of certain actions that can help protect your identity and credit information.

Any laws mentioned herein may not be the same as those in your jurisdiction, so we suggest that you check your state's laws out either online or by talking to an advisor about the one-time fee for placing a Credit Freeze fee that may vary from zero to fifteen dollars depending on your state, your age, and whether or not you have been a victim of identity theft.

A full list of every state's fees at the time of the writing of this book is provided for your reference on our website at:
FreezeOutCrooks.com

● ● ● ● ● ● ● ●

Freeze Out Crooks

Freeze Out Crooks
for
Identity Theft Protection

By Gene Grossman

From

©MMXVII Gene Grossman
All rights reserved

**With special supplements on
Declaring your Residence a Homestead
and popular Internet Fraud Schemes
to watch out for**

Distributed through
FreezeOutCrooks.com

INTRODUCTION

Some time ago a person buying some property from me told me about a law passed here in California that went into effect in January of 2003. If you're curious, it was California Civil Code Section 1785.11.2 (a), but to avoid making your ears glaze over with my reading the thousands of words in that section and all the other related ones that followed, I think that just the first 29 words of the section sums up what they want you to know. It says:

"A consumer may elect to place a security freeze on his or her credit report by making a request in writing by mail to a consumer credit reporting agency."

And here's what I consider to be one of the most important parts of that law... it says:
"In the case of an address change, the written confirmation shall be sent to both the new address <u>and</u> to the former address."

The reason I think that's so important is because identity thieves often try to change your mailing address so that you don't receive notices of their attempts to steal you identity... and by the credit bureaus also sending you the notice, you'll know what's going on and be able to squash it.

The rest of the words are a lot of *legalese*, and go on to define the operative terms being used, and the duties and responsibilities of each credit reporting agency, and you can easily Google it if you'd like to read the Act in its entirety, like I did, and that's what made me think it was a good idea to take advantage of it, so I created a letter that was copied, filled out, and sent in to each of the three major Credit Reporting Agencies, (along with the requested $10 fees in California) and was pleased to find out that not only did they receive my requests, but they each sent me a free copy of my credit report.

I don't know if they still do that or if it was required by law, but either way I thought it was nice of them. The bottom line was that I felt a lot more secure about preventing identity theft... until I started

Freeze Out Crooks

seeing a whole lot of television commercials about credit-theft horror stories that featured a bunch of victims endorsing their services and telling about how one or the other of them saved their lives and their credit... and the most prominent one of those services was named LifeLock, and the commercials and website impressed me so much that I called up their 'Questions' line at (800)416-0599, and was put right through to a very nice gentleman named Brad, who offered to answer the few questions I had about their services... and to start out, I only had two main ones:

First, I told him that my fiancée had already placed a credit freeze on access to her credit report at the three main Credit Reporting agencies, and asked him if that would interfere with her signing up for LifeLock's services... and he told me that it would not.

Secondly, I told him that my I also wanted to join, but that I haven't placed my own credit freeze on yet, and asked if he thought that I should, or if LifeLock would do it for me... and his answer surprised me because he said that if I want to freeze my credit report that's OK, but I'll have to do it myself, because LifeLock doesn't place credit freezes on their customers' credit reports.

Well, from what I understood about the law, especially from those two provisions I mentioned on page 5, and from the advice received from that buyer of my property, I thought that putting a credit freeze on was the best move I could make to prevent any un-authorized attempts to access my credit report... but from what Brad told me, ***that's not part of their service,*** so I started to ask more questions, and I must give both LifeLock and Brad credit, because no matter what I asked, he stayed the same friendly, cooperating guy, and politely and professionally tried to answer each one of them but when he told me that LifeLock *does not stop people from accessing your credit report* like a credit freeze does, that did it for me.

I really appreciated how cooperative Brad was, and have no doubt that all of their customer support people are as nice as he was, but as far as I'm concerned, after thinking it over for a while, I feel that their customer services, website, and television commercials just don't do enough to convince me to spend up to $29.95 every month for the rest of my life, when I believe that having placed my own credit freeze in place will stop all the things that they *'discover'* and notify me about, so that they can then put their experts to work trying to stop the damage that my credit freeze would have prevented right from the beginning.

I didn't call any of the other companies that offer to help protect people's credit, so I don't know if they follow the same plan as LifeLock does, or if they place a credit freeze for you and act as the party to be notified that there's some suspicious activity on your credit file, but even if that's the case, I don't see the benefit of paying hundreds of dollars a year for them to act as a messenger service... I can do my own credit freeze, and save that money.

● ● ● ● ● ● ● ●

Chapter 1
How to Avoid Tickets

You might think a chapter with a title like this one has nothing to do with stopping Identity Theft, but it does.

Like most adults, whenever possible, I refrain from stating my age... but suffice it to say that I've been a member of AARP for a while.

I started driving at the age of sixteen, and successfully collected a large number of speeding tickets during a very short period of time: so many, in fact that at the rather strong suggestion of the Illinois Department of Motor Vehicles, I took a one-year break from driving and became quite familiar with Chicago's excellent public transportation system that ran through the city on all of the main streets that were no more than four blocks apart, and criss-crossed our city very effectively.

When moving to California it was quite evident that compared to the efficient large one in Chicago, the transportation system out here is severely lacking,

Freeze Out Crooks

especially if you want to go anywhere that's not close to a large main street, into nearby towns, into a large tract of residences, or up into the hills... and at that time there were no subways or elevated trains and no Uber or other companies like that.

If you wanted to go anywhere at any time you felt like it, you'd have to drive... and the traffic police had this Victorian policy of actually enforcing the inconvenient laws set forth in the state's Vehicle Code... a set of regulations I'd never even heard of back in Chicago, where the street cops acted like judges and often even collected the fines in advance, thereby saving you the trouble of waiting in line where they're supposed to be paid... a process that the cops here in California apparently weren't taught at the police academy, and became a quite perturbed when one merely hinted at the benefits of it.

Therefore, I decided to change my evil ways and figure out a new way that I could live a long and happy prison-free life out here, and remain an automobile driver instead of a bus rider.

After much thought and consideration I actually succeeded in figuring out the only perfect way to beat the system, drive all over the state, and never get a speeding ticket... and it didn't involve the use of a radar detector or a high-speed chase.

Actually, it was quite simple, and after a while it became sort of a life-style that still works for me to this day... and here's the plan: **I never drive over the legal speed limit**.

And guess what? I discovered that by using my new system in a city with a lot of traffic, that even on an occasional freeway trip, not speeding only might add just a minute or two to my travel time to each destination.

To play it safe, I also got into the habit of starting my trip about five or ten minutes earlier, which improved my reputation for punctuality, and also removed the anxiety of arriving late because of my strict adherence to the law.

And now..., to show you how my ticket-free philosophy applies to protecting the security of

Freeze Out Crooks

your identity, it's as simple as my system for avoiding speeding tickets... and here's the plan: **Stop giving your private credit information away to people that want to help you fight identity theft!!**

Surprised? Well, you shouldn't be, because Identity/Credit thieves are not geniuses: they're just a bunch of immoral crooks that take advantage of your mistakes, and whenever you 'slip up' and do something that makes it easy for them, they're experts at taking advantage of it and exploiting the opportunity.

The bottom line here is this: there is no long list of things you must do to protect your Credit and Identity: instead it's just a short list of one thing TO DO, and several to AVOID DOING.

● ● ● ● ● ● ● ●

Chapter 2
Watch your Luggage

The reason those rules just mentioned exist, is because if you don't follow them you will be put at risk, and that's because your luggage is a lot like your personal credit information and so you should look at it in the exact same way as when traveling long distances on public transportation. And if you think this suggestion is as far out as my system to avoid speeding tickets, think of it this way:

If you have to take a commercial airline to reach a destination, and you have the option of a non-direct flight that will force you to make two stops along the way and change planes – or, a direct non-stop flight that costs a little more, but has no stops or plane changes, please consider spending the extra money for the non-stop flight.

Don't get tempted by the lower cost of taking the two-stops flight: I have a special reason for you to do what I suggest, and that reason is because as I've

Freeze Out Crooks

said just now, your luggage is a lot like your personal credit information.

Yes, I know, your personal credit information is not heavy to carry, but... just like your luggage, the more times it has to be transferred and the more people that have to handle it, the more of a chance you have that it will get lost, and I'm sure you know that travelers' luggage gets lost probably as often as people's credit information does, because the same rule applies to both: **the more people that handle it, the more chance of an error or rare intentional act to misplace, steal, or misuse it**.

I also believe that you don't have to go out of your way to give your personal credit information out to people, because they have ways of getting it that are cleverly designed so that you don't see what their real purpose of asking for it is... and now I'm going to list a few ways that can happen – and please understand that in no way am I implying that anyone asking you about your information is a crook, because there are a lot of online companies that need your information to provide you with useful services that can help you... but you never know who the few bad guys are that also want that information, and can hack the guys you do give it to.

The bottom line here is this: be very stingy when giving out your personal information, and don't hesitate to inquire why they ask for it, if other people in the same business do not.

● ● ● ● ● ● ● ●

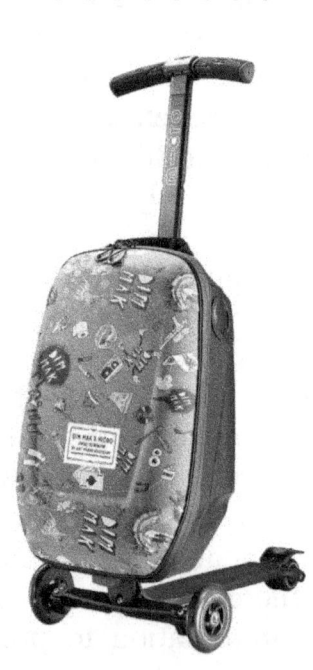

Chapter 3
Happy Birthday

My insurance lady's company sends me a birthday card every year... that's a nice gesture I wish she'd stop doing, because I hate those annual mortality reminders, but I don't want to insult her with a request to stop it, so I just take each card that comes in and file it in the round plastic receptacle under my desk.

Other companies you do business with might also like to add you to their birthday mailing list, but in order for them to do that, they must know when your birthday is, and in doing that they may also ask for the year you were born - and that might be a danger signal, because of all the birthday cards I've sent out over the years, I've never asked for a year of birth. If you know the month and the day, that's enough information to send out a card.

The only exception is if I'm sending one to a child, because they're the only ones that are excited to know that they've just gotten a year older. Unlike us grown-ups, *they* still like that.

Here's aDanger sign: if it's not for some insurance underwriting or for identification purposes on a driver's license or identification badge when age becomes a vital statistic, the only other reason that requires a year of birth that I can think of is for identity theft, because it is one of the main parts of your personal credit information and never should be asked for if only for the sending of a birthday card.

Many times an online entity will request a year of birth for a survey, or other innocent-looking reason that appears to be merely for statistical purposes, but if they already know the month and day you were born and then also ask the range of your birth years of say between 1970 and 1980, once you give them that 'range' information, there are only 10 years you might be born in, so I ask: would you feel safe with a combination lock on your jewelry box that only had ten possible choices to choose from to open the box – and then left that box out in the open? I think not.

Freeze Out Crooks

And now, think of it this way: computer hackers are not usually interested in stealing information from websites that don't have anything they can use or steal.

Some time ago there was a famous bank-robber named Willie Sutton, and during his forty-year career in crime stole millions of dollars... and that was back in the 1920's and thirties, when a million dollars was a lot of money.

Anyway, he was finally caught and sent to prison, where he was interviewed by a reporter who asked him why he robbed banks, and his answer was quite reasonable: he simply replied *"Because that's where the money is."*

And the reason why a lot of websites and online entities get hacked is because of what's now called the *Willie Sutton Rule*: **that's where people's private identity information is.**

It seems like barely a month goes by without us hearing of some large organization that's been hacked, and the result was the theft of credit card numbers, names, customer information, social security numbers, birth dates: all information that can be used for only one reason..., and it's not to help trembling dogs get adopted... it's to steal identities.

The bottom line here is this: Don't worry too much about an online entity that wants your birthdate, but be very careful if they also want the year of your birth too, for some sort of 'survey.'

I have to make a confession here: sometimes I'll come across a website like that, asking for the year of my birth for one reason or another, so I'll give them a birthdate that's not my real one, with a different month, day, and year.

And, as a blatant act of vanity, I make myself at least ten years younger... and am sorry to say that I don't even feel guilty doing it.

If someone who doesn't really need it has the nerve to ask for my age, they deserve to be lied to... and if you don't think I'm right, just ask any female.

● ● ● ● ● ● ● ●

Chapter 4
There's no Free Lunch

If you build a website and want people to know about it, you have to register it with the search engines. Google is probably the biggest and most important one, but there are many others that a lot of people use. Google, Yahoo, and Microsoft are in the top ten, but there are also hundreds more, and there's even a list of the top 300 in that second-tier, and several companies have designed computer-driven systems to include your website's address in all of them.

Some of those search-engine-listing companies offer their services free of charge, but even though you're not paying them a fee, it's really not free because there's a lot of money made in the selling of your email address to online marketers that want to claim that what they send out isn't unsolicited mail, or 'spam,' because they're only sending it out to you because *they're affiliated with a company you've already done some business with*, and they are: they've purchased your email address from a company that you 'gave' it to, when they provided a 'free' listing of your website to a bunch of search engines... who in turn also wanted your email address so that they could then ask you to verify its validity and then sell it to more online marketers.

Other online entities require your email address in order for you to read other pages on their website and get some valuable information about one thing or another, like tips on health, investing, or other great services that you'll be allowed to participate in once you've given them your email address.

An email address is a valuable part of your personal information, and that's why I suggest that you have more than one of them. A private one for all of your friends, family, and people that you do want to communicate with, and another to give out to businesses and people online that request it for allegedly legitimate reasons, which in their mind is the selling of it to other marketers.

Free email accounts are easily taken out with Yahoo, Hotmail and Google, and if you follow my advice and use one or more of them when buying something online or 'registering' to receive some information or any other reason, you'll soon see a tremendous increase in unsolicited messages coming in to that free email account, and because it won't be from family, friends, or people you want to communicate with, you can just ignore it and adjust that account's settings so that all unopened messages are automatically deleted after their minimum-allowed period of time.

The bottom line here is this: If it's not a family member, friend, or other person or entity you want to hear from, don't give away the email address of your private account: use a second email account for the absolute strangers, and even a third account for those you might want to allow to reach you, like for getting an estimate for work done on the house, or a requested cost of some other service, or a person you met while traveling that you wouldn't mind hearing from some time again in the future.

In addition to being annoying, spam costs industry billions of dollars a year. Imagine if a company with 1,000 employees each spend 15 minutes each day just clearing out their spam, that's equivalent to 250 person-hours each day, and if they earn even a minimum wage of $15 and hour, that $3,750 every day – 5 days a week, and can easily come to close to a million dollars a year: and that's from only one company – and that doesn't count the expense if someone inadvertently opens a spam that has an attachment that can plant a virus.

Chapter 5
Free Things Cost Too Much

There are a numerous infomercials on television masquerading as talk show or interviews that feature people that have had a bad experience with their credit: somehow, it was stolen and used by a criminal that obtained their social security number and date of birth.

I also see a lot of scary television commercials that offer things like ability to check your credit score, a month or two of free credit monitoring, a free report on whether or not you qualify for a loan, reverse mortgage, or other type of credit.

These commercials are not 'scary' in the way that horror movies are, but I use that word because they scare the daylights out of me – and the reason they scare me is because for all of the companies that offer those free services to actually provide what they offer, they'll need your social security number.

So, I have to think... what happens to that very personal information after you give it to them. How do they keep it secure after providing you with whatever they promised you, and once you give them the information – if you've subscribed to their continual service – how can you quit it?

Of course there's always some sort of a money-back guarantee so you can get a refund of the money after jumping through all the hoops they place in front of you, but how safe is all of your private information... your name, address, date of birth, credit card number, social security number, and whatever else they've asked you for?

Once you subscribe to a monthly service and provide your personal credit information, they may be one of those services that places a credit freeze on your behalf and list themselves as the person to be notified if there is any apparent attempt to access your credit records for any purpose.

They then notify you that there has been some inquiry about your credit, and you must tell them if the inquiry was authorized or not.

Freeze Out Crooks

You give them an answer as to the legitimacy of the credit inquiry and they then relay that to the credit bureaus.

If the inquirer was known by you, then everything's OK – but if you didn't authorize it, then they refuse to release any info about you and the credit threat is eliminated... and this is exactly what a credit freeze does – but if you do it yourself, the credit bureaus will not release your information unless they're provided with your private PIN, the **P**ersonal **I**dentification **N**umber you're assigned when the freeze is placed on your account.

You contact you directly, and your answer to them is instant: there's no 'middle man' acting as a messenger service between you and the credit bureaus, and charging you every month for that.

The only problem arises when you want to quit using that monthly monitoring service, because remember: they're the ones that put the credit freeze in place, and they're the ones listed to be notified, so that if you want to stop using their services, there's a lot of work to do to have them removed as the notified party and substitute you or whatever new service you're using in their place... and then, what happens to all of that information you gave that monthly-charging service?

Does it stay in their database? If so, where is it saved? Can it be deleted upon your request? What's the process of cancelling the monthly charges to your credit card?

I personally had a cancellation problem like that with an internet 'hotspot' service provider. They cancelled my service as requested, but it took so long for the credit card charges to be stopped that I had to cancel the card... and then, even though they weren't getting any money from me each month, it's now a year later and I'm still receiving an automated text each month telling me that my credit card was successfully charged for another month's service... when it really hasn't been.

Of course I checked my statements and see that I'm not being charged, but their accounting software sure needs some upgrading, and their customer service is non-existent. I hate to mention names, but that company was **Boost Mobile**, and the reviews of their company I saw online warned me that their customer support was practically non-existent, but I stupidly didn't take that advie, so I sure hope they've fixed those problems since my experiences.

But if you do decide to use them (there service is good, it's just the other stuff I wasn't happy with), or any other type of service company like a cellphone service provider, internet provider, or company that you've never heard of before that offers customer support in any way, the best thing you can do before signing up for their services is to simply call their customer support telephone number and ask a question like, "can I pay my monthly fee by a direct deposit from my bank yours?"

I've never come across a subscription service company that will allow that, so I'm pretty sure that if you actually get to speak to a human being that doesn't have too strong of foreign accent, they won't have an answer for you… but not to worry, because in most cases you won't get to speak to a live person before you to through a terribly long series of 'options' to press a key if one applies, and when you find a company like that, then you should think of how tough it's going to get some help when you really have an actual problem, or want to quit... so maybe you should choose to use another service.

And here's another tip you should consider before signing up with a company that you know nothing about: ignore their huge advertising budget for TV commercials and fancy website: If you want to find out about the **ABC Company**, just do one thing: go to Google and type in
    "**ABC Company Complaints**."

A search of the web will instantly bring up what the company's customers may have complained about, and give you a better idea whether or not you might want to sign up and do business with them.

● ● ● ● ● ● ● ●

Your Credit Scores Should Be Free. And Now They Are.
Get your free scores

Chapter 6
Vanity is OK

I've already confessed to lying about my age in Chapter 3, but I have other reasons to lie about it and it's not *just* because I'm trying to hide it... it's because I'm *absolutely* trying to hide it.

That may have sounded a little confusing, but there's more than one reason to hide something: one of them is because you want to lead someone to believe that you're either younger or older than you really are for one reason or another, or you justifiably feel that your date of birth is none of their darn business because that is an important part of your holy grail of private credit information.

There are 'dark' sites on the internet where the bad guys can get your social security number and others that have your date of birth, but it can be a lot of work to find one of those sites that offers both of those items.

That's why the most common item of credit theft is your credit card number... and it's also the one that's the easiest to avoid being hurt by, because once you see a questionable item on the monthly statement, you can contest the charge and have it eliminated.

Personally, whenever a rare event like that takes place, if it's less than a dollar or two, I'll pay it and monitor next month's statement to see if the action is being repeated – and then I'll contest both of the charges because I'll then know for sure that it was done by one of the bad guys... and so will your credit card processor, because they'll agree with you.

Another thing you can do is call the vendor to let them know that they should reverse the charge because it was given to them or entered improperly or that it might be a 'dry run' test for future large unauthorized charges to be made.

And before you ask, please rest assured that the reason I pay the first month's charge is because there are a lot of times when telephone clerks taking call-in orders for merchandise mistakenly enter a wrong number of the credit card being given to them, and I'm concerned that if I report

Freeze Out Crooks

the error and contest the charge, it might be on one of the credit cards that I've given to a vendor for a monthly service like cellphone, internet, domain hosting, or one of the other many places that will have to be notified of a new credit card number.

And if anyone asks for my social security number, I ask why they need it, and if all they can come up with is one of those "Oh, we *just* need it for our records," then I *just* hang up.

● ● ● ● ● ● ● ●

Chapter 7
Living in a Box

Yes, I know, the thought of being forced to live in a box sounds like the terrible fate that many homeless often are forced into, but there is a large number of middle-to-upper-class-people that have done exactly that: they live in a box, but it's not made of cardboard - it's made of metal, and it's very secure, and a good place to receive packages and mail - and it's located in one of the many UPS stores: it's a P.O. box.

They're usually open six days a week until 6:30 in the evening for you to pick up packages that came in for you, and also usually offer services like shipping your packages, a copy machine, a notary public for documents, fax service, and 24-hour access to your mailbox.

The reason I mention the UPS locations is because most of them have actual street addresses that will allow you to make it appear like you're either living there or using it as a business address, by stating the box number as a "suite" number... and this is

Freeze Out Crooks

important when ordering something from a company that refuses to ship to a P.O. box because there's no way to verify that it was delivered... but at a UPS store, there's someone there to receive and sign for it... and if you move, you can still keep the same shipping address for packages if you'll be relocating in the same general area.

Another reason that people like me and so many others have one and use the box number as a "suite" number is because these UPS stores are a very safe place to receive mail and packages, instead of having them left on your front doorstep or near your mailbox... especially during holiday seasons when the news programs broadcast security camera footage of people that make a habit of stealing mail and packages from front porches or areas where they see stuff sit after it's delivered.

But here's the really important reason why a UPS store mailing address is valuable: Anyone looking at your mail that might be lying outside your front door can easily see by the return address on the envelope that the mail is from a Credit Card Company.

Getting a free look at your credit-card statement gives them all they need to steal your identity too... and they don't even have to take the mail: all they have to do is carefully open the envelope, look inside, and copy the important info - and their work is done.

A lot of mail comes from organizations that have your personal identification numbers, date of birth, credit card numbers, social security numbers, and a lot of other valuable private information... and having that information stolen can cost you your identity and credit, and in some cases even your house.

When some credit thief wants to take out a new mortgage on your house without you knowing... he'll first try to change your mailing address so that he can receive notices that you won't know about, but as mentioned in the law cited earlier, you also may get notified of a change-of-address request if you have a credit freeze on, so you'll be able to squash the criminal acts before they have a chance to go into effect.

Freeze Out Crooks

I'm not trying to scare you, but I do want you to know that your incoming mail is like your luggage: the more places its handled, and the more people that handle it, the more chance that something not nice will happen, so take the direct non-stop route, and that's why having your mail safely received by a UPS store or other business offering the same type of services is a smart security move.

I believe many of the UPS stores are independently owned and operated, so the prices of their boxes and the services they offer can vary from store-to-store, so feel free to shop around for the best deal and services.

The UPS box does cost, but just having the peace of mind that your mail, packages, credit and identity just might be a little safer is really worth it... and if you go the way of using a one-time fee service to file your credit freeze (like we'll get into later), the money you'll save each month will more than take care of the cost of the UPS box.

Chapter 8
Stingy is Good

There are very few reasons for any online entity to request your Social Security number, and I can only think of a few:

• An online brokerage house like **E-Trade, Ameritrade**, or another one you would like to open an account with: they must send you important information that will affect your taxes;

• Communicating online with one of the three major credit-rating agencies to request your credit report or inform them of a possible inaccuracy in your credit report;

• Opening up a Bank or Credit Union account;

• To request credit for a purchase or loan;

• Correspondence with Social Security or IRS;

• An organization that will be paying you on an affiliate basis for referrals from your website;

• An organization that will be paying you for merchandise sold to them or services provided;

• An organization that will be paying you royalties or residuals for creative works;

• Any organization that pays you wages or buys your products.

There may be others, but those are the only that come to my mind... but I have a solution that can help reduce the number of people having your Social Security number: it's an EIN: those three letter stand for **E**mployer **I**dentification **N**umber. It's very easy to apply for, the application forms can be filled out online, and it goes to the Federal Government because they issue the numbers.

An EIN won't help you when applying for credit, but if you are a service or product provider, or have a business that receives payment for royalties, residuals, or other reasons, the W-9 forms that people ask you to fill out often offer an option to enter an EIN instead of a Social Security Number, but unauthorized use of that number does not help anyone that wants to steal your credit or identity.

IMPORTANT:
Check with the IRS to see if you and/or your business are eligible for an EIN. At the time of this writing, their information telephone number is (800) 829-4933 but if you're one of those people reluctant to speak to the IRS, all you have to do is

Google "getting an EIN," and you'll easily find out how to apply for your EIN online.

I believe that that the issuance of one only takes a day or so, and the bottom line is this: it's just like other items in your arsenal of private information... in fact, your Social Security number is probably the most important of them all, so be very, very, careful when giving it out, and if you can start using an EIN instead, you'll be way ahead of the identity theft protection game.

And by the way, you should know that having an EIN does ***not*** replace your Social Security Card: it's just an additional way to identify yourself to people that may be sending you taxable income..., so you can still use your Social Security number for all other purposes: just remember to report any income received from your use of the EIN, because it won't appear on earning statements you receive from sources where your Social Security number was used.

And remember: all taxable income must be reported to the IRS, because if you want to avoid going to jail using the same system I use to avoid

Freeze Out Crooks

getting speeding tickets, then make sure you report all money that comes in. There are very few instances in which it doesn't have to be reported [unfortunately, royalties from book sales is not one of those instances], and unless you're collecting on a lawsuit for personal injury, or one of the other rare exemptions, it's probably taxable... and by 'probably,' I mean the IRS will no doubt want you to 'share' it with them.

● ● ● ● ● ● ● ●

s

Chapter 9
Never go Fishing with a Stranger

Here's a very dangerous method that identity thieves use on the internet. It's nickname is 'fishing,' but it's spelled differently than the sport... this one is spelled **P-H**-I-S-H-I-N-G: but it still means the same thing - with one difference: when the word fishing is spelled with the P-H, *you're* the fish... and the crooks want to reel you in just like anyone does when you've got a bite.

And not coincidentally, identity fishing and sport fishing are also similar because they both use bait to attract the fish: you might use something like a worm or a lure as bait, but the identity thief usually has something on the hook that looks a lot better than a worm: like maybe a letter on IRS stationary addressed to you with a warning that you owe some back tax money, and if you don't pay it very soon, you may be arrested, have your wages and savings attached, and also lose your home and car... so you'd better pay up soon – or else.

Freeze Out Crooks

But things are not all that bad, because this time the IRS is going to give you a break and allow you to earn a slight discount on your debt if you start to make payments immediately by credit card... and all you have to do is provide your date of birth and Social Security Number, to make sure that the payment is correctly credited to your balance, and also give your Credit Card Number.

Sounds great doesn't it? A discount on the amount you owe, and a payment plan you can use your credit card on

And that's not where it stops, because it seems that there's also a new phony FBI that has a great program by which many other good things can be accomplished, like expunging your past criminal record, failure to report some cash payments, or other slight errors in judgment you may have made in the past.

The only problem is that these letters and calls are not from the IRS, or the FBI, or from your bank, or from PayPal, or from anyone else that actually exists. The crooks offer letters or websites that look really official, with your name and address on it.

That's right, it's a phishing scam that wants your social security number, and credit card number, and some payment... but other variations on this scheme don't threaten you or ask for money... they simply offer help in making sure that your contact information is correct, so that payments can be sent to you properly.

These *'Correct Your Information'* requests usually come in an email that looks exactly like the bank you're doing business with, or PayPal, or any other organization that you might be doing business with, and look exactly like a very popular successful organization, because they'll send these emails out to a lot of people, and they want to make sure that the email reach people that actually do business with the companies on the letterheads – so they pick the major banks like Bank of America, Wells Fargo, and companies like Amazon, PayPal, eBay, and others like that.

If you've ever received a message like that from a bank that you don't do business with, you probably think that it's an error, and you might even respond calling their attention to the fact that they've sent the message out to a wrong person –but you should **never respond to them** because if you do, you'll be giving them your email address that they already have, and letting them know it belongs to someone that couldn't spot a fake when looking at it, so that they'll know to keep trying with you until one of their scams tricks you - and you fall for it.

I can't count the times that I've received notices that my PayPal account is being suspended because of misuse, and to reverse the suspension I must provide them with personal information so that they'll believe that I'm the correct person to believe when requesting a change to the account... and that was all before I even had a PayPal account!

The bottom line here is this: the *real* IRS, FBI, PayPal, bank or credit union – or any real business you do business with, will *never* send you an email requesting your social security number or any other personal information, like a password, date of birth, or driver's license number – so be careful, and don't give them any gifts.

If you receive a call from one of these fraudsters on your cell phone, look at the incoming telephone number that the call is allegedly coming from, and if it says "Restricted" or any other type of wording that blocks the caller's number, tell them that's someone's at your door and you definitely want to talk to them so they should please give you their call-back number so you can get right back to them after you're done paying the pizza delivery man knocking on your door.

You won't be given a call-back number: they'll just hang up on you and move on to their next potential victim.

● ● ● ● ● ● ● ●

Chapter 10
Electronic Pickpockets

Because identity theft and unauthorized use of credit is such a growing problem, there are companies selling a product that can help you from getting pickpocketed..., but the kind of pickpocket they're offering to protect you from isn't some person that will accidentally bump into you, take your wallet, and then apologize for the bump – this is the pickpocket that's standing near the check-out line with an electronic gadget that's supposed to be able to read the black strip on your credit card that contains all your personal information - from as far as ten or fifteen feet away.

I'm no electronics expert, but in their television commercials I believe they call it something like a *scanner*, that can read your credit information off the credit card that's still in your pocket! I don't know if they can also get the info from the new credit-card chips too, but if it doesn't now, I'm sure that new ones will soon come along that can.

I have no doubt that something like that might exist, but the danger isn't enough to get me to spend 10 or 20 bucks to get a special credit-card wallet that some crook's scanner can't see through while my credit card's still in my pocket, when it would be much easier to read it when I take it out of my pocket, and slide it or chip it through the device on the cashier's counter... and the other reason that turns me off of spending any money for a wallet to protect my credit-card-number is the fact that the people selling those wallets are asking for my credit card number to pay for it.

And even if those electronic pickpockets can get my credit card, what can they do with it? If you've got a card from a reputable organization, they probably have a security policy that protects you against unauthorized purchases so that your liability is either limited or non-existent – and a quick online look at your card's activity will show any use of the card with an unfamiliar-sounding name, so you can immediately call either the merchant (because many have their phone number on the statement), or the credit card company, to protest the charge – and the credit card processor will probably check it out to see if it's one you actually authorized but didn't recognize the official name of the merchant.

Quite often, a person getting your credit card number will do two things before loading your card up on debts:

First: they'll make a charge at a very common place like a Walgreen's Drug Store, in a small amount like less than five dollars. This is done to see if the credit card is still active, but is such a small amount that you'll probably not even notice it on your monthly statement, or if you do see it, think that your wife or one of the kids probably bought something at Walgreen's and forgot to tell you about it.

Second: If that first test works, and the charge isn't contested in the next 60 days or so, the next thing the crooks will do is contact the credit card company to let them know that you would like to change the statement mailing address to a new location... a P.O. Box... and to convince the credit card company that you're really the person that's got the card, they'll ask about that small Walgreen's charge that you believe your little girl made.

Third: They will then wait for your next credit card statement to arrive at the new P.O. box using your name, on which they will see what your card's spending limit is.

If they see something like a 20,000 dollar limit, and your bill is only a couple of hundred, they may send a cashier's check in to pay your bill in full, thereby establishing the new mailing address as being valid, and then go out on a buying spree that uses up about half of the 20 thousand-dollar limit.

When that bill for the 10,000 comes in to the P.O. Box, it will no doubt offer a minimum amount that can be paid, and if that minimum is in the neighborhood of just a couple of hundred, they'll probably also send in a cashier's check for that minimum payment, and then go out and 'max' out the card for the other 10 thousand dollars.

And the card-holders will never know what was going on... unless... they also have an online account with the credit card issuer, that sends out the usual email every month saying 'your statement is available to view,' for people who like to make an

Freeze Out Crooks

immediate payment online... or if the credit freeze that they requested is in effect and they've also been notified of the change-of–address request, in which case this all wouldn't even have been allowed to happen at all.

But: if the cardholder is stupid like I used to be, he or she will probably ignore that message and prefer to get a hard copy of the statement in the mailbox, to send in the payment and check off the deductible items on the bill.

Here's the flaw in that credit thief's plan: If you have already opened up an online account after receiving one of those monthly notices that your monthly statement is available for viewing and paying, that account is still viable even after the thieves changed your snail-mailing address: they couldn't change the email receiving address, because they didn't know it.

It also means you can view your statement and see that first 10 thousand of payment, notify the credit card company that your never got your statement and that the thief probably changed the address, immediately cancel the card and have the mailing address changed back to the real one... yours, and have the credit card company put a red 'flag' on the account, so that when it's used the next time, the merchant will know it's a fraudulent attempt, and follow instructions from the credit card company to hold on to the card and call the police immediately.

<u>The bottom line here</u> is this: if you use one or more credit cards, the next time they send you their customary offers to view your statement on line, if you haven't already registered with to do so online, **please do it now**... and you'll then be able to see your statement not only when they send you a reminder that a payment is due, but you'll also be able to see your statement in real time, indicating every charge made, almost up to the minute – so that if a phony charge pops up, you can notify the credit card issuer immediately, and save a lot of trouble down the road.

The bottom line just mentioned is the good news: the bad news is that many of us have our credit cards automatically charged every month for repeat payments, like rent, internet access, cell phone, car payments, or other types of constant-amount bills. Therefore, you should always keep a list of those automatically paid accounts so that in the event of a credit theft of that card, you can immediately notify those service providers of the new card number and expiration date, so your services will not be interrupted.

In some instances, you might be able to get the same credit card number with a new expiration date, and that will make it a lot easier to change with your service providers... and if you're looking for a tip on how to defeat any electronic pickpocket, you might try what I do: instead of a big fat wallet stuffed into my pants pocket, I leave the wallet locked in my car trunk, and only carry one credit card in my pants pocket, sandwiched in between my plastic Automobile Club card and Kaiser Membership card, so that all the pickpocket might be able to do with scanned information is get a flat tire changed or a free flu vaccination at a Kaiser medical facility.

Of course, if you remember what I've said before in this book, a Credit Freeze should let you know if someone is trying to change the mailing address of your credit-card statement, because if the law in your state that covers what the Credit Reporting

Bureaus must do is anything like the law here in California, they'll probably be required to also send you a copy of the change-of-address request to the old address formerly used... which is where you can receive it.

● ● ● ● ● ● ● ●

Chapter 11
Freeze Out Crooks

There's an easy solution to all of the above situations, and you can do it yourself, because any serious damage that credit thieves want to do can't be accomplished if they can't get one of the three main credit reporting bureaus to go along with it... and I don't mean in a conspiracy, I mean getting the credit reporting agencies to release your credit report, because no lender or provider of credit will do anything with getting a credit report from one of them before granting any credit.

The thieves might try to get away with changing your mailing address on a credit card bill, but you can stop that easily yourself, if you take our advice and establish an online relationship with each one of them... and can also be a great help with your budget planning by knowing in advance how much your next credit bill will be so you're not surprised when it comes in.

And of course a credit freeze will also prevent an unauthorized attempt to change your real billing address, because the law mentioned several times in this book that protects access to your credit reports also requires the credit reporting agency to send a copy of the address-change-request to the new address and also to the old address.

When I sold some property to that out-of-state buyer I mentioned earlier, he was going to be out of town but wanted to make extensive repairs to it, so he trusted me to oversee the repairs, email him the bills and he would authorize an immediate bank transfer of the funds so I could make the payments.

The amount of repairs he authorized came to almost thirty thousand dollars, so I put them on my credit card and used the money he sent me to completely pay off the mortgage on another piece of property I owned... and then began to pay off the credit card balance by accepting the offers I would receive from my other credit card providers that would allow me to transfer balances to them and pay no interest for the first six months.

By ping-ponging the offers I received for no interest during the first six months. After 18 months of three six-month no-interest periods, I was able to pay off the large bill, while accumulating enough air miles to visit a friend in Hawaii.

The reason I'm telling you about this series of events is not necessarily for you to do the same thing, but to lead up to what I discovered shortly after I completely paid off the original big balance:

I learned that the buyer of my property had notified the three credit-reporting agencies that he would be transferring funds and billing them to his own credit cards, so that they wouldn't look at the large charges as being unauthorized – probably to then ping-pong offers that would allow *him* to do the same thing *I* did – but when it was all over, he thanked me and we continued to correspond.

During one of our conversations he told me that he had frozen his credit and suggested that I do the same. At that point I had no idea what he was talking about, so I did some Google research, and as told in the Introduction to this book, found out what he was talking about, and that's why I've written this book: to tell everyone to do the same, because if they do, it'll be a lot harder for the credit thieves to stay in business.

First of all, you should know what a ***Credit Freeze*** is, how you accomplish it, and what it does for you. Its main purpose works the same way that most states' Department of Motor Vehicles do: when someone other than law enforcement or someone licensed to do so runs a license plate number through in a request to find out who the vehicle owner is, before DMV releases the information, they send a notice to the vehicle owner, letting them know that someone is 'running their plate,' and they ask for the owner's permission to release the information. They also tell the plate owner who the inquiring person is.

The three credit reporting agencies act in a similar way, but they do a better job than DMV, because when you request your credit freeze, each of the three credit reporting agencies issues you a PIN – **P**ersonal **I**dentification **N**umber... and here's an example of how it works:

Not too long ago I visited a Verizon store to get a new cell phone and start using their service. Naturally, they asked for my credit card so that they would be putting monthly charges onto it, but they also asked for my permission to run a credit check on me and I gave it to them.

In stores like Verizon, and many other point-of-purchase locations, they do the credit checks while you wait right there in the store, and in about ten minutes they know if they'd like to extend credit to you and complete their sale.

I figured that they'd want to check my credit, and I had already put a freeze on it with all three of the credit agencies, so I brought along a piece of paper will all three of my PIN numbers on it... and sure enough, the salesman came over to me and said that the credit reporting agency wanted to talk to me on the phone, so he handed to me.

The person on the other end introduced himself to me, told me which agency he was with, and asked me to identify myself by telling him my PIN number, for whom I would like the credit report freeze lifted, and for how long the freeze lift should be in effect.

I identified myself properly and authorized him to lift my credit freeze only for Verizon, and the lift should remain in effect until they gave him the report – and then placed back into position as soon as procedure allowed. He understood, followed my instructions, and my credit was approved for the purchase.

The reason I've explained the process to you is for you to see several important purposes the credit freeze serves:

First, it prevents any credit provider from receiving a credit report on you without your authorization... either by personally giving them your PIN or doing so by mail or email. I would never give the salesperson in the store my PIN, so I waited in the store for them to call in and allow me to personally provide the PIN to the credit bureau.

Second, it shows that unlike its title of Credit "Freeze," it does *not* freeze you out of getting any new credit: it only acts to freeze out any person or entity that wants to obtain a credit report on you without your knowledge or permission.

Thirdly, it does not stop you from new uses of your credit, because you can simply 'lift' the freeze

Freeze Out Crooks

any time you want for a period of time, for a specific entity to get a credit report on you... and the reason this is all relevant is because another feature of the credit freeze is that when you first request that it be put in place, each of the three credit reporting agencies receiving the request will usually send you a free copy of your credit report... and very importantly, it prevents thieves from trying to change your billing address, so that when they try to max out your credit cards, you'll know exactly what's going on in time to put a stop to it by letting your credit card company know about it, and most of them have a very liability maximum of from zero to 50 dollars.

As mentioned just now, when the buyer of my property was sending me money for repairs, I was using my credit card to run up a medium 5-figure balance, and was using several other credit cards to pay off the debt... and at all times, each of the credit card companies knew exactly what I was doing, because I saw on my report that as the balances were going up towards the credit limits, and as they were being paid off and on the way down, each of the credit card companies was running monthly credit reports to check on the reduction process.

This told me that those credit card companies are a lot smarter than I thought they were. Once my balance hit the half-way mark of credit limits, my three credit card issuers started to take a keen interest in me, to see what I was spending my money on, how fast I was spending it, and how I started to make payments to reduce the balances back down to zero.

They already knew about the property I owned, and also knew which bank had the mortgage, and how much equity there was in the property – so they could see that the my creditors were sufficiently protected if for any reason I didn't pay off the large balance that I ran up.

They also noticed what I was doing to pay off that large balance, and how I made every payment at least a day or two before it was due, so my credit rating stayed in a very high position.

The bottom line here is that you're not the only one watching your credit: all three of the credit reporting agencies are watching it too... and it's not just because they're nosy... it's because they don't

Freeze Out Crooks

want you to get into trouble, because that puts their credit-granting customers in a bad position, and they don't want that to happen either.

It also showed me that once you have a freeze on your credit, and check your credit card balances online periodically, you've got a lot of protection backing you up and keeping you out of trouble – but first you have to know how to place the freeze, in order for it to work for you.

www.FreezeOutCrooks.com

Chapter 12
Putting on the Freeze

I've talked to several friends and neighbors about the benefits of putting a credit freeze in place and several of them complained that they tried to put a freeze on their credit, but had difficulty in succeeding because their requests were sent to the wrong P.O. boxes, or they couldn't find the correct ones, or their request wasn't done properly.

At first, I was under the impression that they just didn't do things right, but I remembered back to when I put my own freeze on because during all my research into how to go about it, I found numerous addresses and looking back, I now think I was just lucky in having all three requests get to the right places in the required format.

I spent some more time researching locations and seem to have found the three that worked for my neighbors, because they each received their credit reports from all three credit reporting agencies.

I've also learned another one or two things about credit reporting agencies, and have heard of complaints raised by their customers concerning a discrepancy in the calculation and providing of FICO scores, the important numbers that credit-providers look to in their underwriting procedures.

Since its introduction over 25 years ago, FICO® Scores have become the 'gold standard' when it comes to measuring credit risk in the banking, mortgage, credit card, auto and retail industries. 90 of the top 100 largest U.S. financial institutions use FICO Scores to make consumer credit decisions.

I noticed that their website's URL is preceded by the words: **F**air **I**saac **Co**rporation. I also have a ***Discover*** card, and every month when my statement arrives, it also displays my FICO score, and my FICO history.

So that was another reason I didn't need the services of a ***monthly-fee-for-the-rest-of-my-life company*** to monitor my credit... and in most large markets the Discover credit card allows you to also get cash back at the register, doing the double duty of also acting like a debit card.

I was never able to find any example of a form that the three credit agencies wanted to see used by people requesting credit freezes, so I had to design one of my own, and since then it's been working quite well for every one of the people I've assisted, because I seem to have put together the right way to provide the eight or nine items of information they require, plus the proper way to word the letter and request the freeze.

Once you organize the information and documents they require, phrase your letter properly, and send your request in to the correct address for each bureau, after a couple of weeks you might receive a copy of your credit report from each agency receiving your payment and request, plus a PIN [**P**ersonal **I**dentification **N**umber] that can be used to identify yourself when requesting a temporary lifting of the freeze or notify them of a problem.

We've posted the charges every state requests for the placing of a credit freeze on our website at **FreezeOutCrooks.com**

The numbers were accurate at the time of this printing in August of 2017, but to play safe you can always use Google to see the Credit Freeze charges in whatever state you reside.

I would strongly suggest that when making your requests, you add some brief statement on the envelopes, like "address correction requested," or "address service requested," like we have stamped on each of the envelopes we provide to our clients.

Here are another couple of things I suggest you do when sending requests for credit freezes:
• Spend another dollar, or so, or whatever it costs to send it with a signature required;
• Take your requests to the post office to mail them there.

Reasons for these 'tips' are because requesting a signature upon delivery will give you a rapid response letting you know that the request was received, but isn't necessary if you bank online and can easily see that those checks you send in to each of the credit bureaus was paid.

And taking the requests to the post office to mail them will serve several purposes: you can inquire about the address comments on each envelope, get advice on any other additional mail options like insurance and/or signature required upon delivery, and as stated earlier in this book, will reduce to a minimum the number of hands the letter will pass through, keeping in mind that it presents an attractive theft target due to its addressees obviously being the credit reporting agencies, and therefore probably containing valuable personal information.

If you feel that you'd like to have some help with your credit freeze requests, you'd either have to be a close neighbor of mine, or use one of the many popular credit-monitoring services – most of which charge a monthly fee, and others that offer free help, but also have other things for sale... or use the one-time-service-fee organization you can contact at **FreezeOutCrooks.com**

As stated above, use Google to find "Credit Monitors" and you'll have many to choose from. After the next section on the commercial services just mentioned I'll offer my opinion on the upsides and downsides of each one: not specific complaints of actual customers, but general discussion about the decision on whether or not to seek outside help.

Freeze Out Crooks

The important thing to know at this point is that putting a Freeze on access to your credit report is the most important economical move you can make to gain the peace of mind in knowing that you've added the most effective layer of protection you could, and also avoided a monthly charge to your credit card every month for the rest of your life.

Chapter 13
Getting Some Outside Help

There are many reputable companies now that can help you to protect your credit and identity, and depending upon what level of services you select, they do all the work for you, and I assume that they do a good job, so in no way am I going to try and talk you out of using them... but I would like to mention other ways to accomplish the same thing and save lots of money.

At the time of this writing, I believe that the most prominent of these providers is **LifeLock**, and they no doubt come through by providing all the services they promise to offer.

Credit Karma and **Credit Sesame** offer to give you your FICO score free, and one of them also offers to electronically file your taxes at no charge.

As with any other businesses, there are some customers that give great 5-star reviews, and others that are not so satisfied, so maybe it's a good idea for you do your own research: check out all of their websites, look for all the other 'credit monitoring' agencies, read the reviews, and make your decision, or just use Google: Insert the name of the company you're interested in, and simply add just one word to your search of the company: "complaints."

Personally, I don't think that all of the services offered by the monthly-fee-charging companies may provide value for the dollar... and I don't mean to say that they don't perform..., I just question the necessity of those benefits. It's not that those extra services aren't worth the money at all, it's just that I question how necessary they are for the one reason you retain those companies: to protect your credit and identity.

For instance, one of those companies offers to monitor arrest records to let you know if someone is being arrested and trying to lead the authorities to believe that they are you... but I really don't think that's a problem. If your name is a common one like Smith or Jones, there are bound to be people getting arrested that have the same name as yours... but will they have your fingerprints, your date of birth, and your exact face on a mug shot? I think not.

In order to have all three of those markers is actually impossible, but... if a person commits a terrible act like blowing up a federal building, yes, you will most probably receive a certain amount of harassment from the low-educated crowd because of the name similarity, but it'll die down once they see the actual perpetrator's picture on television, and it's doubtful if your credit will be adversely affected... but don't expect to be too successful when calling a restaurant to make a reservation.

Another service that those companies offer is to learn about any unauthorized attempt to access your credit report, and notify you about the attempt, and assist to remedy the situation... and that's a wonderful thing to have, but - also as discussed earlier in this book, that's one of the things that each credit reporting agency does once your credit freeze is in place: they do the same thing the DMV does: they notify you if anyone attempts to access your credit information without being able to give them your PIN... and refuse to give your information out unless you say it's OK, so that solves the problem before it arises.

Freeze Out Crooks

One of the monthly fee companies has numerous endorsements on its page about stuff that they've caught, but looking through the first dozen or two, it looks like they all fall into two categories: people using a member's credit to open up a cell-phone account, or the fact that their Social Security number was submitted by someone... and I believe that the credit agencies notify every person having a credit freeze of those events as well as letting the prospective credit grantor know of the issue.

One company offers several types of insurance for loss of funds through credit fraud and it appears to be backed up by established insurance companies, but as already stated, credit card providers limit your liability in most cases too... without you paying them a monthly fee for the rest of your life.

And, in order for them to be in that position of trust, they must also possess all of your private information... and in view of the many reports of companies being hacked and information stolen, I don't know if I'd like another actor in the part of being me just to relay notifications from the agencies to me, when I could just as easily receive them myself, directly from those agencies, instead of paying the credit monitoring company a fee every month for the rest of my life to act as my secretary and relay information to me.

I've already discussed what the average credit-card-number-thief has to go through in order to make a significant rip-off of many thousands of dollars, but that becomes really difficult for them if you follow my advice, place your own credit freeze in place, see your statements online, and receive notices of any irregularity directly from the credit reporting agencies, without the need to pay a monthly fee every month for the rest of your life.

And similar feelings apply to those organizations that offer free help, whether it be through an app or a website. One of them states that they are so protective of your credit that they never ask for your credit card number.

Big deal. How much more damage can they do with your credit card than any waiter in a restaurant can do with when he takes it and disappears to whatever part of the restaurant out of your line of sight, where the card is processed for payment of the check?

And as for that million-dollar policy one company offers to pay to help you fight against your identity having been stolen, I have yet to see where they've spent one dollar of it – and they've been in business for several years, so either the thieves have gone out of business, or a self-instituted credit freeze is really doing the job of protecting you – and the company you're paying every month is taking the credit for it.

That's sounds a lot like the rooster taking credit for the dawn.

As you may have realized, I've spent quite a bit of time researching this matter, and would like you to know two things:
> **One**:   A really good deal is at
> **FreezeOutCrooks.com****

They provide a DIY credit-freeze kit that contains:

* Three letters properly requesting a freeze on access to your credit, with your name and address already pre-printed on it;

* Each letter is properly addressed to one of the Credit Reporting Agencies;

- Three window envelopes for mailing, with your return address on it;

- Each envelope contains a proper address correction service notice;

- Instruction sheet on how to fill in the blanks on the pre-printed forms and what supporting papers to include;

- A manila file folder for your credit records to be kept in, and absolutely no need for you to provide them with your Social Security Number, date of birth, or a credit card number for the kit: you'll be adding that yourself.

And the one-time $39.95 fee can be paid by either your snail-mailing them your personal or business check, or by requesting that they send you a pre-printed PayPal invoice so that if you want to use PayPal or a credit card, you only give the card number to PayPal, and not to anyone else.

And, once you are a client, you may purchase additional DIY [**Do It Y**ourself] kits at a greatly reduced price for your friends and/or family.

[Here comes the fine print - but it ain't] **

And second - in full disclosure, I'm also the main investor in that company, because I'm so impressed by what it does. In fact, even though I'm not like those billionaires on the popular television show ***Shark Tank***, I still feel like one, because I learned about a service business that looked too good to pass up, so I invested in it.

I also helped create the website, its services, many of my friends and family have used it, and as of this date there has not been one complaint.

[And before you ask: NO, I did *not* charge my family when they used the DIY kits to freeze their credit]

A one-time-only charge for your Credit Freeze kit saves you hundreds of dollars every year for the rest of your life, and that will amount to many thousands of dollars over the years that you'd have been much better off saving for your kids' college education, or your own retirement.

● ● ● ● ● ● ● ●

Chapter 14
Declare your home a Homestead

If you're the type of person interested in avoiding identity theft and are also a home-owner, here's a free preview of what I'll be talking about in a future book about securing your financial assets: it's how to declare your house a Homestead.

All it requires is a legal document that complies with your state's laws and gets filed with your county recorder's office, and we're in the process of preparing one now that will fill the requirements for each state.

Once in force, it helps protect your house and property when times are tough. And if you're a history buff, note that this will in no way get you 40 acres and a mule – or 160 acres... those were homestead deals that expired a long time ago.

Homestead rights don't exist under common law: in May of 1862, President Abraham Lincoln signed the first one into law. That original **Homestead**

Act gave settlers 160 acres of public land. In exchange, homesteaders paid a small filing fee and were required to complete five years of continuous residence to receive ownership of the land.

Since then Homestead laws have been enacted in at least 27 states:

Alabama, Arizona, Arkansas, California, Florida, Georgia, Idaho, Illinois, Kansas, Louisiana, Michigan, Minnesota, Mississippi, Missouri, Montana, North Carolina, North Dakota, Ohio, Oklahoma, Oregon, South Dakota, Texas, Vermont, Washington, West Virginia, Wisconsin and Wyoming.

If you own and live on property in any of these states, you really should consider spending the hour or so it takes to file this type of document. The fee for doing so is nominal, but because different amounts of exemptions apply to different types of people (age, handicapped, married, widow), and different classifications of property (rural, urban) and sometimes all with acreage limits of property, I could never find a form in any stationary store that applied to every state, so I had to design my own for use here in California, and am now in the process of designing others, specifically for each of the states having Homestead laws... and if you're not a research nerd like me, and don't want to wait until I finish designing the forms, it would be a good idea to make the one-time expense: talk to a real-estate lawyer familiar with the homestead rules that apply to you and where your property is, and have it done right so that it properly applies to your home.

The rules vary from one state to another, but homestead statutes are similar in intent. They're designed to preserve family homes that might otherwise be taken in bad times or upon the death of the head of the household. In most instances, this protection is available only if the declaration is filed in advance of such a loss.

A legal judgment resulting from medical bills, business losses or accidents could take a family's savings. But with the safeguards provided to you by homestead statutes, your home and land could be protected up to their state's amount of exemption.

For example, let's say that your home is worth $200,000, and it's in a state that has a $150,000 homestead exemption law and, you still have an existing mortgage of $40,000... and your creditors are demanding $20,000.

In this case, if they attached your house and forced a sale – even if it sold for the full market price of $200,000, the first mortgage would take $40,000, and your homestead exemption would give you the next $150,000 – leaving only $10,000 for the creditor... and after paying all the legal fees and court costs, it would be a loss – so they would not even try to do it.

Please check with whoever does your taxes, but I believe that whenever you recover equity due to a Homestead exemption, you have to apply that exempted amount toward the purchase of another home, usually within six months to a year, or your creditors can demand any additional money over the exemption that you owe them.

Also, some kinds of debts must be honored with or without a Declaration of Homestead, like property tax liens and special assessments.

Failure to pay someone you've hired to make improvements on your house or land can result in a mechanic's lien on your property that can also force a sale of your house to collect that payment, but like any other type of collections lawsuit that threatens to force a sale of your house, the amount of the Homestead exemption and other liens like your home mortgage, will add up to a point that it just won't be economically for the creditor to go ahead with the lawsuit because he won't wind up with enough money to cover his legal costs.

Although the cash value of the homestead exemptions does vary, in most states it gets periodically adjusted upward to keep pace with inflation; that's why, it pays homeowners to keep pressuring their legislators to increase these exemptions as the price of real estate rises.

Fortunately, homestead laws are usually liberally construed by the courts, so it might not make a difference if you own an apartment, mansion, cabin or a tent; it still might qualify as a homestead, provided the dwelling is really your "bona fide residence." And if all you own is a piece of vacant land and haven't built a house on it yet, you might even be able to homestead it as your future home site.

Freeze Out Crooks

In one case, a 161-acre parcel in Texas was judged to be a homestead because the bankrupt owner had shown intent to build by drilling two wells and planting fruit trees. (I can only assume that the landowner was camping out on the property to meet the residency requirements.)

A family is allowed only one homestead at a time, and must "show good faith in their claim." Summer vacation cabins, for example, on which declarations have been filed and accepted, have been taken away for debt payment if the owners already had an existing homestead on their main residency back in the city.

Outbuildings and land that are used by the family for enjoyment or livelihood are generally considered part of the homestead. But adjacent lots — or parcels next to a home that are held for idle investment purposes — might not qualify unless they're gardened, logged, or farmed.

Generally speaking, homestead exemptions apply only to married couples and their families. (Some states do have a "head-of-household" exemption that covers two or more people living as a family unit, provided one person supports the other members of the group).

Should one spouse die, the survivor and any children are protected under the exemption until the survivor dies and the youngest child is of age. And, naturally, the exemption terminates if you sell the property. Claims can be filed on successive dwelling places, but only on one site at a time.

Some states — Alabama, Arkansas, California, Florida, Georgia, Iowa, Louisiana, Minnesota, Mississippi, Missouri, Oklahoma, South Dakota, Texas, West Virginia and Wyoming — even permit a tax credit for homestead property. In these states owners are allowed to deduct some set amount from their yearly property tax assessments.

If you're among those folks that live in a state that recognizes the Declaration of Homestead, you'd be wise to get in touch with your county clerk or recorder right away for complete information about the procedure. Filing the document is well worth the few dollars and the little time it requires. It's a simple step that could save you money and it just might even save your home.

Chapter 15
Some things to know about Homestead protection:

1. There is no homestead protection in Maryland, New Jersey, and Pennsylvania;
2. States like Arkansas, Florida, Iowa, Kansas, Minnesota, Oklahoma, South Dakota, and Texas have no limit on the protection… it's unlimited there;
3. Other states like Alabama, Kentucky, Ohio, and Virginia have only $5,000 in protection;
4. The homestead designation applies only to the declarant and in some states your spouse and/or children in their minority years. The homestead designation does not apply to a surviving spouse if remarried;
5. Homestead does not deter your bank from foreclosing if one does not pay the mortgage;
6. As of the most recent adjustment in 2013, the federal homestead exemption is $22,975, so you may be able to select whether you'd like to be under the Federal or State regulations

7. And, just like the bankruptcy rules, if you try to abuse the Homestead exemption in a fraudulent way to get out of paying outside debts, it won't work. Your paperwork must be in order and filed in a timely fashion – and **not** 10 minutes *after* you've been notified that your creditors are after you.

The figures below may be changed, depending on the state you live in, so please find someone in the real estate business that can help you out, should you have any questions... and note that depending on the size of your screen, some state laws may be continued to a following page, and were believed to be correct at the time of this writing, in August of 2017

JURISDICTION	HOMESTEAD EXEMPTION AND STATUTE
Federal Bankruptcy Exemptions	$20,200 -- 11 U.S.C. § 522(d)(1)
Alabama Homestead	$5,000 / $10,000 -- Ala. Code § 6-10-2, 27-14-29

Freeze Out Crooks

JURISDICTION	HOMESTEAD EXEMPTION AND STATUTE
Alaska Homestead	$67,500 -- Alaska Stat. § 09.38.010
Arizona Homestead	$150,000 -- Ariz. Rev. Stat. § 33-1101A
Arkansas Homestead (continued on next page)	**Unlimited** for married and head-of-household residents (but once homestead attaches, not destroyed by death, divorce, or dependents' emancipation) -- Ark. Const. art. 4
California Homestead	$50,000 single / $75,000 head of household / $150,000 over 65 or disabled. -- Cal. Civ. Proc. Code §

JURISDICTION	HOMESTEAD EXEMPTION AND STATUTE
	704.730
Colorado Homestead	$45,000 -- Colo. Rev. Stat. § 38-41-201
Connecticut Homestead	$75,000 -- Conn. Gen. Stat. § 52-352b(t)
Delaware Homestead	$50,000 -- 10 Del Code Ann. § 4914(c)(1)
District of Columbia Homestead	Unlimited -- D.C. Code § 15-501(a)(14)
Florida Homestead	**Unlimited** for 160 acres rural or 1/2 acre urban. -- Fla. Stat. Ann. §§ 222.01, 222.02, Fla. Const. Art. X, § 4.

Freeze Out Crooks

JURISDICTION	HOMESTEAD EXEMPTION AND STATUTE
Georgia Homestead (continued on next page)	$10,000 single / $20,000 married -- Georgia Code Ann. § 44-13-100(a)(1). Note: S.B. 133, which would raise the exemption to $50,000 / $100,000, was reported favorably by the Senate Judiciary Committee on 3/1/07
Hawaii Homestead	$20,000 / $30,000 for head of household or over 65. -- Hawaii Rev. Stat. § 651-92(a)
Idaho Homestead	$100,000 -- Idaho

JURISDICTION	HOMESTEAD EXEMPTION AND STATUTE
	Code § 50-1003
Illinois Homestead	$15,000 -- I.L.C.S. §§ 5/12-901; 5/12-906
Indiana Homestead	$15,000 -- Ind. Code Ann. § 34-55-10-2(b)(1)
Iowa Homestead	**Unlimited** for 40 acres rural, 1/2 acre urban. -- Iowa Code Ann. § 561.16
Kansas Homestead	**Unlimited** for 160 acres rural or 1 acre urban. -- Kan. Stat. Ann. § 60-2301
Kentucky Homestead	$5,000 -- Ky. Rev. Stat. Ann. § 427.060
Louisiana Homestead	$25,000 -- La. Rev. Stat. Ann. §

Freeze Out Crooks

JURISDICTION	HOMESTEAD EXEMPTION AND STATUTE
	20:1. La. Const. Art. 12:9
Maine Homestead	$35,000 / $70,000 if minor dependents. -- 14 Me. Rev. Stat. Ann. § 4422(1)
Maryland Homestead	None
Massachusetts Homestead	$500,000 and $500,000 for each age 62+ or disabled person. -- Mass. Gen. L. Ch. 188 §§ 1, 1A
Michigan Homestead	$30,000 / $45,000 if 65+ or disabled. -- Mich. Comp. Laws Ann. § 600.5451(n)

JURISDICTION	HOMESTEAD EXEMPTION AND STATUTE
Minnesota Homestead	Up to 160 acres. $750,000 rural; $300,000 urban. Minn. Rev. Stat. Ann. § 510.01.
Mississippi Homestead	$75,000 for 160 acres. -- Miss. Code Ann. § 85-3-21
Missouri Homestead	$15,000. -- Mo. Ann. Stat. § 513.475
Montana Homestead	$100,000 -- Mont. Code Ann. § 70-32-104
Nebraska Homestead (continued on next page)	$12,500, limited to head of household. -- Neb. Rev. Stat. §§ 40-101 to -108
Nevada Homestead	$350,000 -- Nev.

Freeze Out Crooks

JURISDICTION	HOMESTEAD EXEMPTION AND STATUTE
	Rev. Stat. § 21.090(1)(l)
New Hampshire Homestead	$100,000 -- N.H. Code Ann. § 480:1
New Jersey Homestead	**None**
New Mexico Homestead	$60,000 -- N.M. Stat. Ann. § 42-10-9
New York Homestead	$50,000 -- N.Y. Civ. Prac. L. and R. § 5206(a)
North Carolina Homestead	$18,500 / $37,500 married -- N.C. Gen. Stat. § 1C-1601(a)(1)
North Dakota Homestead	$80,000 -- N.D. Cent. Code §§ 47-18-01, 28-22-02(7)
Ohio Homestead	$5,000 -- Ohio Rev. Code Ann. §

JURISDICTION	HOMESTEAD EXEMPTION AND STATUTE
	2329.66(A)(1)
Oklahoma Homestead	**Unlimited** for 160 acres rural, 1 acre urban. -- 31 Okla. St. Ann. § 2
Oregon Homestead	$39,600 -- Or. Rev. Stat § 18.395
Pennsylvania Homestead	None
Rhode Island Homestead	$300,000 -- R.I. Gen. Laws § 9-26-4.1
South Carolina Homestead	$50,000 per owner; $100,000 maximum (adjusted for inflation each July starting July 2007) S.C. Code Ann. § 15-41-30(1
South Dakota Homestead	**Unlimited** for 160

JURISDICTION	HOMESTEAD EXEMPTION AND STATUTE
	acres rural, 1 acre urban -- S.D. Cod. Laws § 43-45-3
Tennessee Homestead (continued on next page)	$7,500 unmarried / $12,500 unmarried 62+ / $20,000 married and one spouse 62+ / $25,000 married and both spouses 62+. -- Tenn. Code Ann. § 26-2-301
Texas Homestead	**Unlimited** for 100 acres rural (single) / 200 acres rural (family), 1 acre urban. -- Tex. Const. Art. XVI, §§ 50, 51; Tex. Prop. Code §§ 41.001 to 002

JURISDICTION	HOMESTEAD EXEMPTION AND STATUTE
Utah Homestead (continued on next page)	$20,000 / $40,000 married -- Utah Code Ann. § 78-23-3
Vermont Homestead	$75,000 -- 12 Vt. Stat. Ann. § 2740(19)(D)
Virginia Homestead	$5,000 -- Va. Code Ann. § 34-4
Washington Homestead	$125,000 -- Wash. Rev. Code § 6.13.030
West Virginia Homestead	$25,000 -- W. Va. Code § 38-10-4(a)
Wisconsin Homestead	$40,000 -- Wisc. Stat. § 815.20
Wyoming Homestead	$20,000 -- Wy. Stat. Ann. § 1-20-101

● ● ● ● ● ● ● ●

Freeze Out Crooks

The bottom line of this entire brief book is that protecting your identity and your credit is a lot like crossing the street: if you don't look both ways before crossing, there's a good chance that you'll be hit by a car.

And the same thing goes for credit protection: if you don't monitor your credit, and secure releasing of your credit report with a **Credit Freeze**, and periodically check your credit card statement on-line, there's a good chance that you'll be hit by a credit thief.

There is no reason for you not to have a freeze on your credit, and if you own a home, there is no reason for you not to have it homesteaded.

It makes no difference whether you pay a lawyer or a credit protection company every month to do all the work for you, or you do it yourself: the most important thing is that you do it, so please - get online and check out the free, one-time fee, and all the monthly fee services to make your decision... and if you go with a monthly fee place and want to leave them, you'd better ask in advance if that's possible – and if so, how it affects your credit if you leave them and go to a different company or decide to take over the monitoring on your own... and by so doing, you'll have an idea of what their customer service is like, and whether it's easy or hard to get an answer.

● ● ● ● ● ● ● ●

Chapter 16: APPENDIX
Most popular internet scams

I've talked about **ph**ishing scams earlier in this book, so if you're already wise to those, or the phony letters from you bank, the FBI, the IRS, and that prince in Nigeria, here are some other ones that you should watch out for... and when that disabled Medal of Honor war hero and father of nine begs you for money to help pay his rent, tell him you'd rather send a check made out to his landlord, and that you'll need his mailing address, and not just a post office box.

And if you think what they're doing is a lot of hard work for the small amount of money they probably make, you're way off base, because the reports indicate that in 2106, the scammers took 13 Billion dollars out of America's pockets... and that's only the amount that was reported and verified, so it doesn't include the ones too embarrassed to admit and report it.

No matter how many scam variations there are, they all fall into several main categories:

√ - **Free service**: installing malware in your computer to do not-so-nice things to you and others;

√ - **Imposters**: supposedly from the IRS, FBI, PayPal, your bank: all requesting secure information;

√ - **Frauds**: Nigerian Princes, money transfers, employment, romance, stock tips;

√ - **Fakes**: doctors with health cures, cosmetic wonders, weight loss secrets;

√ - **Criminals**: child pornographers, prostitutes, money laundering, employment offers, romance.

The two things that they all share is a sense of urgency, and a slight grain of truth as to why it is being offered to you, with a semi-logical reason why normal channels can't be used.

A Free One-month Trial:

Be very careful with the cosmetic and health products that offer a free one-month supply of their product: they will ask for your credit card and enroll you in a continual supply of that product unless you return the unused portion and ask to be removed from their automatic charging list.

If they don't ***receive*** your product return and/or request for withdrawal of the 'program,' you'll have one heck of a time stopping that charging and the shipping.

You've won the Lottery!

Of course you don't remember buying a ticket to this particular lottery, but that's okay, because it's one of those special ones that doesn't need tickets: winners are selected by a random drawing of something like email addresses or telephone numbers. And the good news is the money is ready to be sent to you as soon as the 'processing fee' is paid – and that can be any amount from hundreds to thousands of dollars, depending on how hard they think you bit down on the bait.

Guaranteed Approval for a Loan or Credit Card:

This is great: due to your satisfactory efforts in rebuilding your credit, you've earned a spot on the major credit-reporting-agencies' honor roll and now qualify for a loan and/or credit card... as soon as you pay the customary annual fee in advance for the credit card or loan processing.

Gene Grossman

Please Use our Approved Shipper:

You are offered full retail price for whatever you are selling, like merchandise on your website, a used stereo, or anything else, but they will require you to use their shipping company because it's the only one you trust... and just to make sure the shipping cost with their shipper is competitive, they tell you to get a quote from Fedex, UPS, or DHL – and that's what their shipper will charge.

All you have to do is let them know the amount: they will then send you their check for the shipping costs, plus another fair amount for your time, and ask you to send an advance payment to the shipper, who will then make an appointment to pick up the merchandise that they will also pay for in full before shipping.

The check or money order you receive will be phony, but the money you sent to the shipper wasn't... and when their check bounces, you'll realize you sent the money to the crooks and they're now in the wind.

Our other Customer will pay you:

The $3,500 of merchandise you're selling, so because they have heard that you are an honest person, they will trust you, and you will be paid for your merchandise by one of their customers right here in the U.S. that owes them $5,900.

All you have to do when you receive that customer's cashier's check for $5,900 is immediately send them the overpayment amount of $1,400 and then ship the merchandise at your earliest convenience.

Process our Payments:

You are offered a nice job: process payments of their U.S. customers. They will send you their checks, you deposit them, and once they clear, you are to send the money to them and deduct your financial representative fee of 15%.

But – before they can be allowed to trust you to handle their money, they must check your credit, but not to worry: they absolutely do not want one cent from you for their efforts... all they want is information they need to check your credit, prepare your employment contract, and steal your identity.

Happy Birthday!

You have received a birthday card from an old classmate whose name you don't recognize. The card is in an attachment that you'll have to open – and when you do, you'll see a birthday card, but at the same time a virus will be planted in your computer that will do things that are not-so-nice, like:

• Capture you contact list to send spam and malware to them, making it look like it came from you;

• Hook your computer into their illegitimate network of computers that send out spam;

• Install a key-capture virus that notifies them every time you use your credit card, and allows them to capture your credit card and shipping information for their own use;

• Install a program that allows pop-up ads from their sponsors to appear on your computer;

• Disable your computer and offer to release it if you pay them a ransom.

[large companies with customer databases that contain private info are targets for this one: they pay ransom so that customers never learn that they're info was hacked]

You Have Been Infected!

Don't be fooled by this free offer to analyze your computer, find the virus, and clean up your computer so that it runs faster and better.

This is just another trick to get you to download a worthless program… that will be worthless to you, but very valuable to them, because then they can do all the not-so-nice things just mentioned.

*****

Give till it Hurts:

Every time there's some disaster, there will despicable people that try to make money off of it, so don't let it play on your heart strings, because if it's a new charity you've never heard of, it probably doesn't exist outside of the scammer's mother's basement.

To discover whether or not a charity is on the up-and-up or not, there are some websites that can help with your research, and CharityWatch.org looks like it does a decent job.

Always ask what percentage of money actually reaches the charity itself, and where the charity publishes their distribution of funds statistics.

Two new ones to watch out for

The 'call me back trick:'
You receive a voice mail that's meant to make you believe it's from someone you'd probably like to speak to, like your doctor, accountant, stock broker, police officer, etc., etc.

The message will sound very professional, like it's from the secretary or assistant of one of those people you'd like to speak to, and it asks you to please call back at this private-line number.

The problem is that once you make the call to what appears to be a local number, your call is instantly forwarded to another phone number that in some way starts charging you for every minute of conversation... so don't return any call to anyone that doesn't leave a name and reason for you to call that sounds like it's genuine.

The next one is the 'oops' trick:
In this scam, when you answer your phone you hear a person sound like she dropped something and is calling out for you to hold on for a second. When she returns to the phone, she apologizes, and claims that she dropped something off of her desk, and asks you if you can hear her now, and asks if "it sounds OK to you."

Because you probably have a 'courtesy' reflex action built in that makes you respond with something like, "sure it sounds just fine."

Freeze Out Crooks

At this point she'll say something that sounds a little strange to you because you don't know how it relates to the very few words you've both exchanged at this point: she says "Oh, I'm glad you agree with me that it sounds OK to you…" and then she goes on with her sales pitch about something you're totally not interested in.

At this point you probably don't see what the scam is, but if they had obtained your credit card from another source, you might start seeing something like a $9.95 charge appearing every month on your credit card statement that looks like it's for some official –sounding service… and that what the phony call was about: to trick you into saying "sure, it sound just fine" because if you contest the charge, they will respond by playing the part of your conversation when she asks how that sound to you, and you respond that it sounds fine, and she says that she's glad that you agree with her… leading the credit card processing company to believe they're listening in to a recorded part of your conversation where you're agreeing to subscribe to their monthly service… and you'll have a tough time getting those charges cancelled.

I've heard of people that have been forced to claim that their credit card was lost, just so that they could get a new card with a different number that the scammers don't have... and you know the inconvenience that can cause – and those credit monitoring companies with their wonderful staff available to assist you only give you the same info that you've just received for free right here, leaving all the work for you to do, because they're like the rent-a-cop security guards you see: they have no authority to take any action to stop crime... all they do is stand there as a deterrent. Their only responsibility is to observe and report: the heavy lifting is all up to you.

I've personally been targeted by one of the phone scams briefly mentioned above.

Not everyone knows that 1111 Constitution Avenue Northwest, Washington DC is the full address of where the head office of the IRS is located, but quite a few people can probably recognize (202) as the area code for Washington DC and, that's exactly what showed up on my cellphone when a call came in from there.

I saw it on the phone as I was stepping out of the shower, so I just let it go to voicemail because I don't know anyone in DC – and the caller did in fact leave a message.

It sounded like a computer-generated script and it informed me that I was accused of fraud in my tax return by not reporting some income, and that it was urgent that I call them back to stop any criminal action against me.

I recognized it as a scam and ignored it, after sending a copy of it to the IRS fraud division. I included it in the audio version of this book.

Protecting yourself when making online purchases:
Being reluctant to give my credit card number to online merchants that don't offer an address of any physical location, I often have used PayPal as a method of payment.

That method worked quit well with merchants that accepted it as a payment option, but the downside is that I wasn't satisfied with their payment protest process when it came to the shipment of inferior or non-working products, or the complete failure to ship at all.

With most credit cards, you call a number and protest a charge for certain reasons, and I've used that occasionally when the vendors tried to 'subscribe' me to their service on a continuing monthly basis.

I finally figured out the safest way to operate by using a credit card online: ask you bank to open up a separate account and give you a Debit card for the new account that requires the account to be funded for payment to be authorized, and then whenever you want to order something online, simply transfer money into the debit card account that's just a few dollars over the amount of the purchase, so that the vendor never has your credit-card number, and can't make any unauthorized charges to it in the future.

This may not sound like such a great deal for a large percentage of one-time purchases, but there are a lot of companies offering free trials of their product on television. The only catch is that you

Freeze Out Crooks

must give them your credit card number for the shipping and handling charges, and if you don't notify them within the free trial period the you don't want to continue receiving the stuff, you'll learn that it's not as easy to cancel out as they say it is, and you'll be spending a lot of time being jerked around by their alleged customer service department telling you that they didn't receive your timely cancellation notice.

I hate to sound like a worry-wart: there a lot of really good, honest merchants on the internet and you may never come across a dishonest one, but boy... if you ever do, you'll be glad you prepared yourself for it properly.

● ● ● ● ● ● ●

Chapter 18
IMPORTANT NOTICE ABOUT CREDIT CARDS IF YOU'RE A MERCHANT

If you are an online credit card merchant and receive an order for products that are to be shipped to a foreign country, or the order was made without any negotiation as to quantity pricing Be Aware that it might be an un-authorized order, using a stolen credit card number.

Therefore it's important that you're familiar with your credit card processor's contractual rights, because if you accept an order of several thousand dollars, it clears, you will receive an authorization number, and all the money is deposited to you bank, you're still liable for a charge-back if the true card-holder disputes the purchase in a reasonable amount of time after receiving a statement and noticing the charge as being unauthorized.

This means that if it was an unauthorized purchase, the amount paid to you will be withdrawn from your bank account, and you will not receive any credit for the processing fee – and you've already shipped the merchandise!

This doesn't mean that you should refuse large orders from foreign customers, but you might be better served by informing the customer that you prefer to be paid by American Express Money order sent by snail mail.

They're usually available just about anywhere in the world where a large order might come from, and if the customer tries to wriggle out of paying by that way, it's a good sign that you might be getting scammed.

You might also ask for advance payment by a cashier's check from the customer's bank... and by also telling the customer that shipment will not be made until the check clears.

Believe me, there are a lot of people out there all over the world that are placing large orders to people just like you, paying with stolen credit card numbers, and getting a lot of merchandise to sell... so watch out if they also ask you to add soap and/or toilet paper to the order, because those are a rare commodity in some areas of the areas where a lot of fraudulent orders can come in from.

A friend of mine was a foreign correspondent, and stays in touch with many of his former cohorts still active. He tells me that once a week, a special squad of police go through Heathrow Airport in London, and if they see someone near where the international flights come in sitting there for too long, they will ask if that person is waiting for a Prince to arrive from Nigeria... and very often it is a person that has been swindled and is waiting for their prince to arrive with that suitcase full of money for them.

● ● ● ● ● ● ● ●

Chapter 19: Closing Comments

This was a very short, non-fiction book to tell you about some credit and identity protection that I personally use and recommend to others:

My regular efforts at writing have been dedicated to a popular series of books that feature the exploits of a lawyer that wins all of his cases due to the behind-the-scenes work of his 13-year-old legal ward, an adorable little Chinese girl named Suzi that's really the brains behind most of his legal efforts: she's part child and part Sherlock Holmes.

I've written 20 novels that chronicle their work, and if you're curious, I'd like to detail some of them for you on the following pages... where they're all available in Printed books, eBooks, and now as Audiobooks. There are fifteen Peter Sharp Legal Mysteries, and also five of the spin-off Suzi B. Mysteries, so if you're ready to match wits with a 13-yr.-old to see if you can solve the crimes before she does, then please start reading them. They're all set forth in more detail at:

LegalMystery.com

The Peter Sharp Legal Mysteries

About the Author

Gene Grossman worked his way through high school, college, and law school as a shoe salesman, welder, process server, bail bondsman, tire changer, saloon piano player and 'extra,' appearing in numerous motion pictures, while working his way through high school, college/s and law school.

He then spent 20 years as a trial lawyer, during which time he served as Dean of a small local law school, where he also taught several classes on Legal Writing, to help prepare his students for the California Bar Exam.

The film and video company he started while working in the motion picture industry produced over fifty special interest DVD titles on everything from boating, to bankruptcy.

Now retired from the practice of law, Gene writes aboard his yacht, the ***MAGIC LAMP***, in Marina del Rey, California, where he's now working on more stories in his new series: ***the Suzi B. Mysteries***, a spin-off of the ***Peter Sharp Legal Mysteries***, in which Suzi B. takes on cases all by herself – but Peter and Myra always seem to get pulled into the action as unwilling assistants.

If you've ever vacationed is southern California and visited Marina del Rey, you may find some familiar locations in this series of books, because the plots all take place where the author also lives... but it's definitely **not** autobiographical: the book's hero lawyer is 20 years younger, five inches taller, and has a full head of hair.

Gene Grossman

Four covers from the 15-book series of Peter Sharp Legal Mysteries

(www.LegalMystery.com)

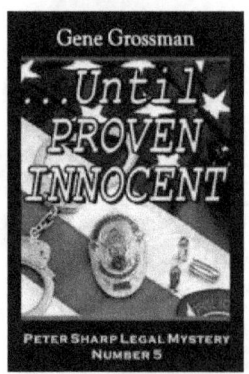
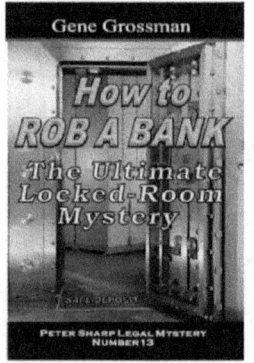

#1: *Single Jeopardy*

Attorney Peter Sharp has been wrongfully suspended from the practice of law and thrown out of the house by his soon-to-be ex-wife, a newly appointed deputy district attorney.

As a result of the eviction, he's forced to live in their back yard on an old, poorly wired, 40-foot Chris Craft cabin cruiser he's restoring, that is in danger of burning up at any time.

To make matters worse, as the result of trying to help someone fill out some claim forms, he gets arrested for conspiracy to defraud an insurance company.

His alleged co-conspirator, a man charged with murdering his own wife to be with a beautiful flight attendant, is about to discover that Peter is also sleeping with her while the man is out of town.

As Peter fights to get his law license reinstated, he discovers the secrets behind two murders, a fatal plane crash, and who framed him with the State Bar - all with the help of his legal ward Suzi, an adorable, quiet (at least to Peter) ten-year-old Chinese girl and her huge Saint Bernard. Peter also gets involved in matters concerning sexual harassment, vexatious litigation, double jeopardy, and a groundbreaking case of Negligent Nymphomania.

● ● ● ● ● ● ● ●

#2: ...*By Reason of Sanity*

In his second Adventure, Attorney Peter Sharp gets retained to defend a man accused of capital murder.

The only things making this case a little harder to defend than most others are that the client's acts were captured on videotape, he confessed to the police, and he wants to plead guilty. To make matters worse, the District Attorney's office has brought in a special prosecutor for the trial: Peter's ex-wife Myra.

Freeze Out Crooks

While he's preparing for trial on the murder case, Peter is also hired to represent an insurance company, to defend it against a man who slipped and fell while inside a bank that was coincidentally robbed later that same day. Peter thinks the case would have died when the claimant was murdered, but at usual, he's wrong.

In this adventure, while Peter is involved representing Vinnie, the prolific, peeing pornographer, he also helps solve several bank robberies by catching the entire gang, and makes the acquaintance of a new friend who runs an autopsy store - all with the help of his legal ward, the adorable thirteen-year-old Suzi and her huge Saint Bernard.

● ● ● ● ● ● ● ●

#3: *A Class Action*

In his third Adventure, Attorney Peter Sharp is retained to represent a man accused of murder, by the planting of bombs in vehicles.

The client is also suspected of being part of a conspiracy to assassinate the President of the United States in an upcoming Fourth of July parade. With the assistance of his legal ward Suzi, Peter cracks the case, identifies the real murderer, and at the same time solves the mystery of a dead body found in his friend Stuart's automobile trunk... all while falling for a lesbian lawyer, winning a Will contest, breaking up a stolen car ring 4,000 miles away, and battling with his ex-wife, who has been elected to the office of District Attorney.

In the adventure's finale, Suzi miraculously manages to get 'Bernie,' her huge Saint Bernard into a courtroom, where she makes her first official court appearance, holds her first press conference, and becomes a local television hero.

●●●●●●●●

#4: *Conspiracy of Innocence*

Suzi once again saves Peter's case by finding the connection between two crimes that allegedly took place in different parts of the State, one of which Peter was arrested for.

And once again, Peter falls for a woman who he thinks could really 'be the one' this time. Peter's ex-wife Myra must make the decision as to whether or not she should resign from prosecution of a case in which she may have a conflict of interest – Peter's murder charge.

Everyone including Peter is sitting on the edge of their chairs as this double murder mystery comes to a shocking conclusion that involves a mafia hit man, revengeful drug dealers, a local police chief, and the ever-popular FBI.

● ● ● ● ● ● ● ●

#5: ...Until Proven Innocent
[Winner of the 2011 Global eBook Award – **Fiction: Mystery Category**]

Tony Edwards, A dock neighbor of Peter's, is charged with murder.

Unfortunately, he is a suspended police officer with a known dislike for people who are the color of his alleged victim. He's also the subject of many citizen complaints for using excessive force in the minority community.

At Suzi's request, Tony has taught her how to help him re-load his target practice ammunition, also giving the little girl a basic course in ballistics. When a local black movie producer who Tony was working for gets killed, Suzi and talks Peter into handling Tony's defense… which doesn't look too good because he was arrested at the scene of the murder with his gun still smoking.

Along the way, Peter once again gets involved with who he thinks might be 'Miss Right,' represents a 500-pound woman who is being discriminated against, uncovers a white supremist militant organization, and also stumbles onto a group of people who are pirating DVD copies of recently released major motion pictures.

Peter's ex-wife, District Attorney Myra Scot, makes a mistake when she subpoenas little Suzi to come and testify as a prosecution witness against the defendant, Suzi's friend Tony. After what Suzi does to solve the mystery and destroy Myra's case in court, everyone knows that the D.A.'s office will never subpoena Suzi again.

● ● ● ● ● ● ● ●

#6: *The Common Law*

Peter Sharp encounters a client with amnesia, who not only can't tell Peter what his own name is, but who also has absolutely no recollection of the crime he is charged with committing.

Freeze Out Crooks

In lieu of his memory, Peter's obtains video surveillance footage that establishes his client's guilt beyond a reasonable doubt.

The usual crew also gets involved, including Peter's close friend Stuart, Jack Bibberman the investigator, Laverne the 'amorous houseboat lady', and Stuart's employees Vinnie and Olive – who are having some disagreement as to whether or not they're legally married; and last but not least, little Suzi B. and her big Saint Bernard.

The law firm is still operating from their 50-foot Grand Banks trawler yacht in Marina del Rey, California... the vessel that Peter still doesn't know how to drive.

The ***Suzi B***.

As in past adventures, all involved continue to visit the local haunts. One way or another each of

Peter's cases winds up being a conflict with his ex-wife Myra, who is the county's chief prosecutor. He also may be more closely involved with FBI Special Agent in Charge Bob Snell than before, as they share a dangerous high-speed situation on a winding road. Suzi's new friend Lotus and her mother also play an interesting part in this adventure as Peter finds that he is fighting a ring of credit-card fraud experts.

● ● ● ● ● ● ● ●

#7: *The Magician's Legacy*

In this seventh adventure, Suzi decides that she wants to study magic. Unfortunately, her teacher is the main suspect in what appears to be an 'impossible' crime... the shooting of a man in his completely locked 'safe room.'

In order for Suzi to clear her magic teacher of liability for this crime, she must convince Peter to handle the case, which he does under one condition: Suzi must help him by solving the mystery of this locked-room murder. Her task is made difficult because all events took place in a secure 'panic room,' with steel doors in place, and no windows.

Somehow, the alleged murderer is believed to have committed the crime and successfully escaped from a room that could only later be opened by a crew using blowtorches. Suzi is especially motivated to solve this enigma when she learns that an attorney who she dislikes may be involved.

● ● ● ● ● ● ● ●

#8: *The Reluctant Jurist*

There's a mini flu epidemic going around in Los Angeles and it has especially taken its toll among Superior Court Judges in Santa Monica, who all seem to have been infected at the same conference they attended.

Peter has been 'drafted' to fill in as a temporary judge for some civil matters, but winds up getting stuck hearing a big criminal trial involving a previous attorney as the defendant... the same attorney who Peter crossed swords with in a previous situation.

Suspense enters the picture when Peter's legal ward Suzi fails to appear as guest of honor at her own birthday party, and every local state and Federal peace officer in California wants to locate her.

This is the second adventure that Peter and Suzi B. have been involved in where Suzi's Saint Bernard may be partly responsible for a successful conclusion.

●●●●●●●●

9: *The Final Case*
Suzi dislikes a certain devious attorney who Peter keeps coming up against.

When Peter's new romantic interest invites him to a cocktail party, Suzi and the other guests are shocked by a loud noise down the hall, coming from their host's study.

Other guests at the party include the chief of police, mayor, and district attorney, who unanimously conclude that the dead body they discover is the result of a suicide.

Even Suzi is inclined to go along with their conclusion... until she learns that the devious attorney she dislikes may be involved in handling some legal matters for the deceased.

Suzi won't let go of this one. Against everyone's advice, she keeps working to prove her suspicions about that devious attorney and his connections to what Suzi believes must have been murder.

#10: an Element of Peril

In the tenth ***Peter Sharp Legal Mystery***, Peter faces a double task: defending a person who is charged with murder, and also trying to locate the missing victim, who was allegedly killed in a completely locked room.

Somewhere behind the tangled mess of a downward-spiraling celebrity starlet, a battling married couple, a missing currency trader and a disappearing corpse, attorney Peter Sharp and his legal ward Suzi must find where the truth lies.

As in the past, while Peter's client's trial nears, Suzi fails to come up with any workable solution that can save Peter from certain defeat and humiliation in court.

You'll be sitting on the edge of your chair as you see the courtroom drama that takes place during the last few minutes of the trial.

● ● ● ● ● ● ● ●

#11: *A Good Alibi*

In Latin, the word "alibi" literally means "somewhere else," and to any person charged with a crime, it is an extremely valuable asset to have because it can mean the difference between an acquittal and a conviction.

However, just having an alibi isn't enough: it has to stand up to scrutiny, because any good prosecutor knows that breaking an alibi and proving it was fraudulently concocted can lead a sure-thing conviction.

In this eleventh adventure of the Peter Sharp Legal Mysteries, Peter is drawn into a role he never thought he'd be playing – that of a prosecutor, being brought in as for the singular purpose of trying to break a defendant's apparently 'airtight' alibi.

● ● ● ● ● ● ● ●

#12: *Legally Dead*

Nobody likes a killer, but when you're a trained professional called upon to do a job, you have to put your personal feelings on hold.

When attorney Peter Sharp's former wife Myra calls to ask a favor, he finds it difficult to refuse her,

Freeze Out Crooks

because any occasion to work with her is always a pleasure for him.

The favor that District Attorney Myra asks is for Peter to represent a client in court who wants to plead guilty to a crime. A plea bargain the defendant agreed to is already in place.

Peter agrees to the contemplated one-hour of work as a court-appointed defense attorney and makes the court appearance. But when the case is called, the surprises start, and don't stop until the unexpected end of this twelfth of the Legal Mystery series, during which time Peter gets his first opportunity to defend a dead person charged with murder.

● ● ● ● ● ● ● ●

#13: How to Rob a Bank

There are many types of mysteries, but one kind stands out over all the others: the ones involving a Locked Room.

Over the years, every mystery writer worth his salt has tried to come up with one that tops all the rest: the secret compartments, doors locked from the inside, confused timelines, etc., etc.

It's all been tried over and over. Jacques Futrelle set the standard with his Problem in Cell 13, and

John Dickson Carr raised it a bit in his The Hollow Man, but there haven't been many fine stumpers since then... until now.

Mystery writer Gene Grossman has been a fan of locked room mysteries for many years, so when he created this 13th Peter Sharp Legal Mystery, it was natural for him to want to include what may be one of the most baffling locked room mystery of them all – but maybe with exception of Book #7: ***The Magician's Legacy.***

In this story, a magician is writing a book entitled "How to Rob a Bank," and to get publicity for its upcoming publication, the author decides to show the public that he really knows of what he writes – so he plans to rob the bank he regularly does business with.

Unfortunately, things don't work out the way he planned, and it takes little Suzi to solve this baffling mystery for all of the adults.

● ● ● ● ● ● ● ●

#14: *Murder Under Way*

Author Gene Grossman, an admitted fan of locked room mysteries has attempted to 'jump the shark' with this fourteenth book in the Peter Sharp Mystery Series by creating a locked boat mystery.

Freeze Out Crooks

Peter's dock neighbor was found dead in his boat, fifteen miles offshore, just minutes after having placed an emergency S.O.S. call to the Coast Guard.

There is apparently no way that any person could have boarded his boat, which was travelling at 30 miles an hour, shot him, and escaped the boat, without having been noticed on radar or search helicopters, so the victim's death was classified as being a suicide... until Suzi decided it was murder.

Join Peter and his friends as they explore the quaint City of Avalon, on Catalina Island, the favorite vacation destination for Southern California boaters, and see if you can figure out the solution to this mystery before Suzi can.

● ● ● ● ● ● ● ●

#15: The Sherlock Holmes Caper

It's no secret that attorney Peter Sharp is a huge fan of the Sherlock Holmes stories, and that fact has been seized upon by a person who has an evil agenda in leaving a series of clues behind, each somehow relating to one of Arthur Conan Doyle's Holmes stories.

Gene Grossman

When the District Attorney's office finally figures out that the clues relate to Holmes stories, they call the only Holmes expert they know of who can help them figure out what the clues are an indication of – a crime that has already taken place, or one that is about to take place.

● ● ● ● ● ● ● ●

Little Suzi   Big Bernie

Editor's note:

If you happen to notice any blatant typographical errors in the text of this book, we suggest you bring them to the attention of the author, who was the last person to sign off on the manuscript.

We feel quite comfortable shifting the blame onto him for any errors he may have missed. He can be reached through us at...

Editor@MagicLampPress.com

Please be sure to put the word "FREEZE" in the subject line of our email, so we'll know which one of our authors to forward your message to.

Gene Grossman

Celestial Navigation for the Complete Idiot: A Simple Explanation
[Winner of the 2011 Global eBook Award – **non-fiction Sports category**]

This book is ground breaking not only because of what it has, but what it doesn't have:
> No complicated drawings;
> No mathematics problems;
> No astronomical talk;   and,
> No big words you've never heard of.

Sailor-author Gene Grossman finally breaks this wonderful subject down into plain English and explains it in such a way that you will no longer

Freeze Out Crooks

have any excuse to claim that you know nothing about the valuable boater's subject of Celestial Navigation.

This book was inspired by Gene's DVD program of the same title, which has gained worldwide popularity and is being used by Navies, Coast Guards and sailing schools all over the world.

● * ● * ● * ● * ● * ● * ● * ●

In closing, I want to thank you for reading this book, and hope that your credit stays safe and intact for as long as you desire... and never, ever give your social security number or credit freeze PIN number out over the internet before getting the requester's name and phone number, to call and make sure that it's really your bank, the FBI, or the IRSs... which it probably isn't.

But not to worry, because no matter who you ask, they will immediately hang up on you, because they ain't who they say they are... and won't want to waste any time with someone they believe is on to them.

Gene Grossman

Gene Grossman

More Books by the author

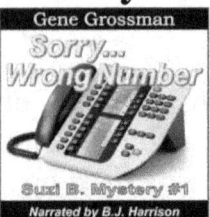

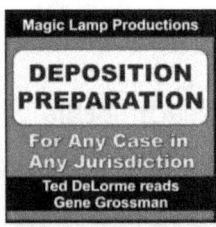

All described at **LegalMystery.com**

Freeze Out Crooks

From Wikipedia, the free encyclopedia

A **credit freeze**, also known as a credit report freeze, a credit report lock down, a credit lock down, a credit lock or a security freeze, allows an individual to control how a U.S. consumer reporting agency (also known as credit bureau: Equifax, Experian, TransUnion) is able to sell his or her data. The credit freeze locks the data at the consumer reporting agency until an individual gives permission for the release of the data.

Today, credit freezes are made possible by state laws as well as industry-initiated rules. Laws have been passed by nearly all the US states (see partial list below). The first state to pass a credit freeze law was California, with SB 1386 sponsored by Debra Bowen in 2003.

In late 2007, all three of the major credit bureaus (following TransUnion's lead) announced that they would let consumers freeze their credit reports, regardless of the state of residency.

State laws still apply, however, in instances where the cost or other details of the freeze are more favorable than they are under the industry-sponsored alternative.

Gene Grossman

* * * * * * *

The **homestead exemption** is a legal regime designed to protect the value of the homes of residents from property taxes, creditors, and circumstances arising from the death of the homeowner spouse. Laws are found in state statutes or constitutional provisions which exist in many states in the United States. The homestead exemption in certain southern states has its legal origins in colonial Spanish exemption laws. Exemption laws in other states were enacted in response to the effects of economic health in the 19th century.

Different jurisdictions provide different degrees of protection under homestead exemption laws. Some only protect property up to a certain value, while others have acreage limitations. If a homestead exceeds these limits creditors may still force the sale while the homesteader may keep a certain amount of the proceeds of the sale.

California protects up to $75,000 for single people, $100,000 for married couples and $175,000 for people over 65 or legally disabled. In California, SB 308 was introduced in early 2015. It initially proposed a $700,000 homestead exemption

Freeze Out Crooks

regardless of age or marital status. It has recently been amended down to $300,000.

Texas, Florida, Iowa, South Dakota, Kansas, and Oklahoma have some of the broadest homestead protections in the US, in terms of the value of property that can be protected.

Texas's homestead exemption has no dollar value limit and has a 10 acres (4.0 hectares) exemption limit for homesteads inside of a municipality (urban homestead) and 100 acres (40 hectares) for those outside of a municipality (rural homestead). The rural acre allotment is doubled for a family: 200 acres (81 hectares) can be shielded from creditors in Texas for a rural homestead.[1]

Both the Kansas and Oklahoma exemptions protect 160 acres (65 hectares) of land of any value outside of a municipality's corporate limits and 1 acre (0.40 hectares) of land of any value within a municipality's corporate limits. Most homestead exemptions cover the land including fixtures and improvements to it, such as buildings, timber, and landscaping.

New Mexico has a $60,000 exemption.[2] Alaska has a $54,000 exemption.

Colorado has a $75,000 exemption or $105,000 for people who are over 60 or disabled.[3]

Gene Grossman

In the majority of states, the real dollar value of "protection" provided by these laws has diminished as exemption dollar amounts are seldom adjusted for inflation. The protective intent of such laws, with some notable exceptions stated above, has been eroded in most states.

A homestead exemption is most often only on a fixed monetary amount, such as the first $50,000 of the assessed value. The remainder is taxed at the normal rate. In that case, a home valued at $150,000 would then only be taxed on $100,000; a home valued at $75,000 would be taxed only on $25,000.

The exemption is generally intended to make the property tax a progressive tax. In some places, the exemption is paid for with a local or state (or equivalent unit) sales tax.

● ● ● ● ● ● ● ●

Editor's note: all figures mentioned above are those of Wikipedia, and should not be taken as the law. Check with an expert in your state first.

Freeze Out Crooks

A ready-to-use CREDIT FREEZE kit for a one-time-only service fee and then no monthly payments forever

We print your NAME and ADDRESS in and then all you do is fill in the blanks and mail them to the 3 Credit Bureaus

It's that easy

I've made what I believe to be the best and most economic suggestions for you to follow in an effort to give your credit and identity the most protection, like ...
- Banking online and checking your account frequently;
- Using a UPS store to receive your packages and sensitive mail;
- Having more than one email account for private and public use;
- Paying for online purchases with either PayPal or a special-account debit card;
- Using Google to check for complaints against any businesses you're not familiar with;
- Putting a Credit Freeze on access to your credit report at all 3 credit bureaus;
- Not falling for some online scam for a *free* credit score or credit assistance;
- Using the Discover card and their free FICO score and Social Security Number scanning services;
  and,
- Checking your credit-card activity online for unauthorized purchases - plus all the other suggestions in this book.

So whether you use *our* Credit-Freeze package or not, please at least take my advice and protect yourself as much as you can, and thank you very much for reading this book.

www.ingramcontent.com/pod-product-compliance
Lightning Source LLC
Chambersburg PA
CBHW071440180526
45170CB00001B/394